The Visibility Hack

The Visibility Hack

One Book Can Transform Your Personal Brand & Business

Ousha Demello

The Visibility Hack
One Book Can Transform Your Personal Brand & Business

Ousha Demello
ISBN: 978 1 7391878-6-6

Publisher: The Uplifted Publishing
Cover & Book Interior Designed by The Uplifted Publishing
Edited by The Uplifted Publishing

This book is dedicated to the visionaries, the entrepreneurs, the quiet experts, and the bold storytellers all around the world.

To those who have lived through experiences that shaped them...

Who carry within them a story, a skill, a passion, or a mission that the world needs to hear.

To the coaches, consultants, creatives, and founders who are ready to stop hiding and start leading— Not by shouting the loudest, but by standing in their truth and letting their story do the talking.

This is for you—the ones who know deep down you're meant for more. Who are ready to leverage your voice, amplify your impact, and finally be seen as the authority you already are.

Your story is your power.
Your book is your breakthrough.
This is your visibility hack.

Ousha Demello

Table of Contents

"You don't need a bigger audience. You need bolder positioning."

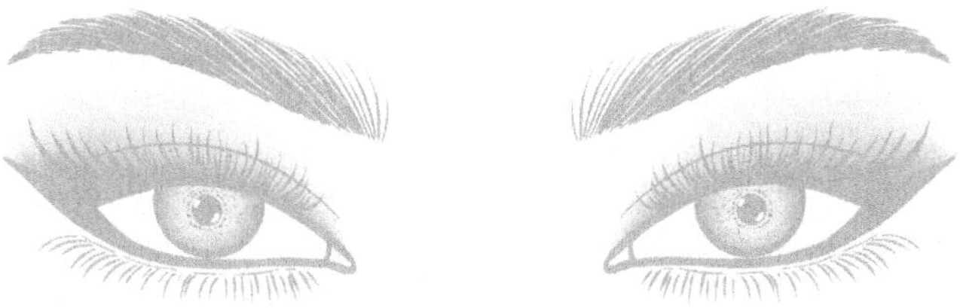

Introduction

INTRODUCTION

"You don't need a million followers.
You need one good book."

In today's world, the battle for attention has never been fiercer. Everywhere you look, from social media feeds to email inboxes and podcasts to conferences, people are shouting, sharing, and selling.

Standing out isn't just important anymore; it's essential.

Without visibility, even the best ideas, products, or services risk being lost in the noise. Now, you might be thinking: In a world saturated with TikToks, reels, status updates, and AI-generated content, isn't writing a book kind of outdated?

Well, this book will show you how to cut through the noise, build authority, and create a long-lasting personal brand by writing one powerful book—even if you're not a writer, don't know where to start, and feel like no one is listening. Visibility isn't just about being loud or everywhere; it's about being seen by the right people, in the right way, at the right time.

It's about crafting a message and presence that resonates deeply and authentically. That's why having a book as part of your visibility strategy is a game changer. They might be more powerful now than ever before.

And the truth is, "books still change lives".

Why?

Because in a distracted world, people crave depth. They want something real. Something lasting. Something human. And a book—your book—offers exactly that.

A well-written book doesn't just educate or entertain; it conveys authority, credibility, and permanence. When you hold a published book in your hands, people see you differently. They see an expert, a leader, someone with a message worth listening to.

In a marketplace flooded with content, a book gives you a real, lasting edge. While posts fade and videos get buried, a book has gravity—it pulls people in. It stays. It speaks when you're not in the room.

Think of your book as your greatest asset—not just for visibility but for legacy, connection, and growth.It makes an IMPACT:

- Influence
- Message
- Positioning
- Authority
- Credibility
- Trust

I – Influence: A book multiplies your impact beyond your reach. Your book becomes your silent ambassador, working for you 24/7 in rooms, inboxes, and hearts. It puts your voice in rooms you haven't entered yet and in the hands of people who need to hear from you—even when you're asleep.

M – Message: A book is an extension of you, your message, and your brand. It enables you to convey your approach, philosophy, and story in a way that resonates deeply with your audience. The good thing is that writing a book forces clarity. It pulls your ideas out of the clutter and crystallises your voice. It helps you define not just what you know but what you believe—and why that matters to others. It's your worldview, crafted with intention.

P – Positioning: In a noisy market, a book is your signature. It separates you from dabblers and puts you in the realm of trusted experts and thought leaders. It's your calling card, your proof of concept, your credibility anchor. Conference organisers, media producers, and collaborators see authors as serious players.

You don't just "do the work"—you own your space.

A – Authority: Being a published author automatically elevates your credibility. It signals dedication, discipline, and depth. Readers and clients trust people who create something lasting—and nothing lasts like a book.

C – Credibility: Media outlets, podcasts, conference planners, and clients often ask one question: "Have they written a book?" Why? Because they trust books more than any other content format. Why? Because books take time. They take thought. And most of all, they take heart.

A book instantly positions you as credible, trustworthy, and intentional. In many industries, it's still the gold standard for media and professional recognition. The very act of writing one sets you apart from the crowd.

"Anyone can post a reel. Not everyone can write a book."

T – Trust: This is the biggest one. Readers trust authors. A book says, "I've walked through something—and I've made sense of it. Now, I'm offering that to you." Your book invites people into your world in a deeper, more vulnerable way than any post or podcast ever could. And that emotional connection? It stays with them.

So let me ask you:

What would change in your life or business if the right people finally saw and understood your message?

And just as importantly—what's the cost of staying invisible for one more year?

If you've been quietly dreaming of writing your book, one that reflects your truth, elevates your visibility, and transforms your business, know this: that dream isn't just possible. It's powerful. And it's time.

And if you are still wondering: "Do I really need a book when there's already so much content out there?"

The answer is simple: Yes—because your book makes an IMPACT that lasts.

In a world flooded with short-lived content, your book does what no reel, post, or podcast can do on its own. It builds your credibility. It positions you as the authority. It deepens trust. It expands your reach. It becomes a lasting expression of your message, your method, and your mission.

This book will guide you through the process—step by step.
Because your story doesn't just deserve to be told.
It deserves to be read, remembered, and respected.
So, are you ready to stop dreaming about writing that book and actually make it happen?

Let's take that first step together.

— Ousha Demello

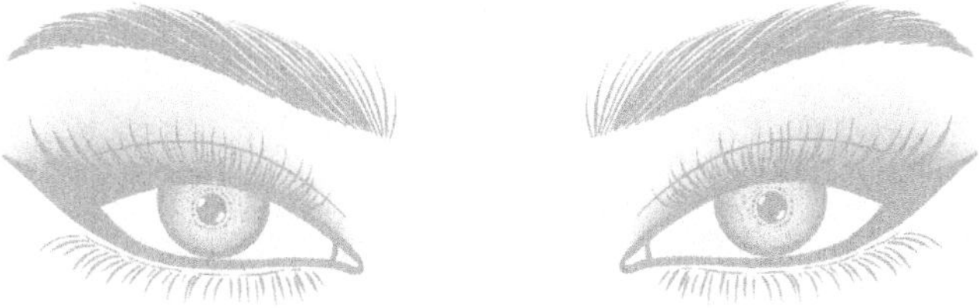

Chapter 1

It's Not Your Fault... Until You Do Nothing About It

It's Not Your Fault... Until You Do Nothing About It

If you're holding this book, I already know something about you:

- You feel the pull to share your story.
- To make your voice heard.
- To create something lasting.

Maybe you've been carrying the idea of writing a book for months—perhaps even years. You've probably told yourself, "I'll start when things slow down... when I feel ready... when I have more time or more clarity." However, the truth is that the book still hasn't been written. I get it. Not because I studied it but because I lived it.

For years, I silenced my storytelling, thinking it wasn't the right time, that no one would care, or that I wasn't qualified enough to share my words with the world. But once I started writing, everything changed. My healing deepened. My confidence grew. And doors I didn't even know existed began to open.

Writing a book is not just about content. It's about courage. It's about taking what you've lived through—your wisdom, your struggles, your wins—and turning it into something that matters. Something that leaves a mark.

And yet, if you're like most people I've worked with—business owners, creatives, speakers, professionals—you might be feeling blocked, overwhelmed, or even afraid. You know you have something to say, but something keeps stopping you from saying it.

That's where we begin.

Before we discuss structure, strategy, or publishing, we need to address what's truly getting in your way. Not the surface-level stuff—but the silent struggles no one talks about. The ones that keep smart, capable, passionate people stuck.
This next section is going to be honest.

It might even feel a little uncomfortable.

That's good.

Because discomfort is often the doorway to clarity. Clarity is the first step toward writing the book that's already inside you.

Let's examine what's holding you back—so we can move through it together.

THE 7 SILENT STRUGGLES KEEPING YOU FROM WRITING YOUR BOOK

1. "I'm not a writer."

You've convinced yourself that writing a book is for "other" people—people with degrees in literature, big platforms, or perfect grammar.
But let me tell you something: The world doesn't need more writers. It needs more truth-tellers. Your story, your experience, your voice that's what people need. You don't need to write like a novelist. You need to write like you.

2. "I don't know where to start."

You've got so many ideas, memories, lessons, and messages, but how do you turn that into a book?
What goes first? What do you leave out? What if it's all a mess?
You're not alone. Most brilliant people drown in their own brilliance because they lack a simple roadmap to guide them.
Good news? This book is the roadmap.

3. "Who am I to write a book?"

Imposter syndrome. The voice in your head that whispers:
"You're not successful enough."
"No one wants to hear your story."
"You're not special."

Let me be blunt: That voice is a liar. And worse, it's stealing opportunities, connections, and legacy from you every single day you stay silent. You don't need to be perfect to be powerful. You just need to be real. One of my mentors, once said,

"You don't need to be great to start;
you need to get started to be great!"

4. "I don't have time."

Between your business, your job, your family, your never-ending to-do list... when are you supposed to write a book? But here's the truth: You don't need more time. You need structure, support, and a system. You need to stop trying to do it someday and commit to a process that makes it possible now.

5. "What if no one reads it?"

You're afraid you'll pour your heart out... and it'll go unnoticed. That you'll hit publish and hear crickets. This fear keeps you small. But here's the shift: You don't write for everyone. You write for someone. One person who needs what only you can say. And that one person? They're worth it.

6. "I don't know what to say."

You've lived a big life. You had big wins. You felt deep pain. But how do you turn your story into something that teaches, inspires, and sells?

That's what I'll show you—how to turn your lived experience into powerful, purposeful content that positions you as an expert and moves the hearts of your readers.

7. "I'm scared."

Scared to be seen.
Scared to be judged.
Scared to put your name on something permanent.

I get it, but writing a book isn't just about sharing your thoughts. It's about standing fully in your truth. What I've learned is that fear doesn't go away; it just gets louder if you don't take any action.

Now, imagine holding your finished book in your hands just months from now, feeling a deep sense of pride and accomplishment as you've finally shared your unique story with the world. Picture yourself waking up each day energised and confident, knowing you have a clear, simple roadmap guiding your writing journey, transforming overwhelm into focused clarity.

Imagine the excitement of connecting with your readers, those one or two people who resonate deeply with your truth and feel genuinely seen and inspired by your words. Visualise the freedom of breaking past fear and doubt, standing fully in your authentic voice, louder than ever before.

See yourself mastering a sustainable writing process that suits your life, bringing balance rather than stress. Envision the doors opening, new opportunities unfolding, and conversations and legacies shaping the future because you chose to speak your truth.

You will feel unstoppable, powerful, and deeply fulfilled, knowing your book is not just written, but alive, making a meaningful impact in the world.

If this is where you want to be, then keep reading because it's time for a smarter strategy. A smarter, more powerful visibility hack that positions you as the go-to expert amplifies your influence and draws the right people to your brand.

This book will guide you step by step through the ultimate visibility hack: writing a book that not only shares your story but also positions you as the go-to expert in your field. A book that not only changes your life but amplifies your influence and attracts the right people to your brand.

Because your book isn’t just a product.
It's your message.
Your truth.
Your platform.
Your legacy.

WHY NOW IS THE BEST TIME TO USE A BOOK FOR VISIBILITY

Books offer something unique: depth and credibility. A blog post or video can capture attention briefly, but a book creates a lasting impression. It enables you to tell your story fully, share your unique insights, and foster a lasting relationship with your audience over time.

Plus, today's publishing landscape is more accessible than ever. You no longer need a big publishing house or a large budget. With modern tools and strategies, you can write, publish, and distribute your book on your terms, quickly and professionally.

Here are some more reasons why writing a book is worth it, especially now:

- Books Are Still Power in a Digital World

You can scroll past a blog post. You might like a reel. But a book? A book demands attention. It invites your reader into a deeper connection with your ideas, your experiences, and your transformation. It positions you as someone who didn't just "have an opinion"; you had the discipline to build and share something of value.

When someone reads your book, they're saying, "I'm willing to sit with your thoughts, your experiences, your story." Especially in today's hyper-speed attention economy, that kind of permission is rare and valuable. Don't you think?

Especially if you're a business owner, coach, consultant, or knowledge expert, one of the most powerful things you can do is write a book. Not just any book, but the right book. A book that captures your wisdom shares your unique process and draws the right people to your business like a magnet.

Your book becomes your powerful business card, your credibility anchor, your silent sales force. It's your voice when no one's asking questions. And for many of us, it becomes the door opener to new opportunities we couldn't even have imagined. I know this firsthand: my book didn't just open doors; it created entirely new rooms I never knew existed.

- Have Knowledge or Experience? You Need a Book

You may have been running a business for years. You could have led teams, solved complex problems, or built things from scratch. You've failed. You've succeeded. You've learned more from the hard days than the good ones.

Guess what? That knowledge? That experience? That's your story. And people need it.

Your book isn't just about where you've been. It's about who you've become and the value that journey holds for others—clients, peers, partners, or the next generation of entrepreneurs.

In a sea of "experts," a book distinguishes you as someone who's done the work, not just talked about it. When written well, it becomes a tool to grow your brand, secure media coverage, land keynote speaking engagements, attract high-calibre clients, or even launch new streams of income.

- Authorship Is a Catalyst for Credibility and Legacy

People respect authors. Period.

It's almost instinctual. When you tell someone you've written a book, their perception of you changes instantly. You're not just someone in your industry; You become a source—a guide.

Whether you're a coach, consultant, entrepreneur, creative, or expert in your field, your book can become the centrepiece of your business. It can elevate your entire positioning. You automatically become a thought leader. It builds authority without you having to say a word. In rooms full of experts, the person with the book is often the one who gets the speaking slot, the consulting contract, or the media interview.

But more than that, it becomes your permanent platform. It captures what you stand for, what you've overcome, and what you've built. It's the part of you that keeps speaking, even when you're not in the room. That's what legacy looks like. It's not ego—it's impact multiplied.

- What Becoming a Bestselling Author really Means

Let me clear something up: becoming a bestselling author is absolutely possible —and you don't need to be famous, rich, or traditionally published to do it. And you certainly don't need to wait.

But here's what it's not: it's not about ego. It's not about gaming Amazon rankings or inflating preorders. Yes, hitting a list is a milestone, but actual bestselling authorship means your book made a meaningful impact. It connected. It moved someone. It helped them see a path forward.

That's the kind of impact I help my authors create. Throughout this book, you'll see real examples—authors I've worked with who've gone on to become #1 Amazon Bestsellers. You'll see their wins, their breakthroughs, and what happened after their books went live.

Because at the end of the day, your book isn't just a goal—it's a gateway. To bigger opportunities. To deeper credibility. And to people wanting to work with you before they've even met you.

THIS BOOK IS FOR YOU IF:

- You know your story and experience could help someone, but you're not sure how to put it into words. You want a roadmap for transforming your life lessons into a message that resonates with people and establishes you as a trusted voice in your space.
- You've built a business, career, or body of knowledge, and you know—deep down—it deserves to be shared, remembered and passed on. You want to turn what you know into something that outlives you.
- You're tired of chasing opportunities and constantly explaining who you are and what you do. You want your book to do the talking for you—to open doors, create conversations, and attract the right people without you having to always be "on."
- You've posted, spoken, or shared online, but you're starting to wonder if your voice is just getting lost in the noise. You want to create something lasting. Something solid. Something that carries your name and your message long after the scroll stops.
- You've seen others step into the spotlight people with less experience, less depth, and less heart, but they're out there, getting the recognition you know you've earned. You're done playing small.

- You've walked through hard things. And now, you want those struggles to mean something not just for your healing but for someone else's freedom, clarity, or inspiration. You want your pain to have a purpose.

- You don't just want to write a book. You want to create a movement. A message. A ripple effect. You want to leave behind more than just content. You want to leave a legacy.

- You feel something pulling at you. A whisper that says, "It's time." It's time to stop waiting. It's time to stop doubting. Time to start writing.

MY STORY

I never planned to be an Author. I never imagined I'd become a consultant, either. If you had told me this years ago, I would have laughed. My journey didn't follow a straight path; it zigzagged through pain, confusion, and moments where I didn't know if I'd ever find solid ground again.

There was a time when my life seemed to be falling apart. I found myself in an abusive relationship that nearly killed me. For me, the mental and emotional toll was far worse than battling physical abuse. I felt isolated, powerless, and alone, as though the world was closing in on me. Every day felt like a struggle, and I often questioned my worth, thinking I'd never find a way out.

But I survived.

Rebuilding wasn't easy. I had to own my story, not just the "good" parts, but the messy, uncomfortable, deeply human parts too. But I realised that survival wasn't enough. I had to heal, to find strength within myself that I didn't even know I had. There were many days when I didn't know if I could make it. I had to ask for help, swallow my pride, and embrace vulnerability. I had to shed the layers of ego and pride I had been holding onto and find strength in humility. That journey was long and painful, but it marked the beginning of my transformation. I had to reclaim my life, my worth, and my sense of purpose.

For 15 years, I worked as a business lecturer, teaching others how to succeed in the business world. Yet, despite my knowledge and experience, I found myself struggling. Every single month, my bank account seemed to be stuck in the red. The stress of working full-time, trying to be the best mother I could be to my baby, and keeping up with life's demands was overwhelming. There were nights when I couldn't sleep, my mind racing with worries about bills, my career, and the future. It took a heavy toll on my health. I felt like I was drowning, constantly on the edge of burnout, with no clear path forward.

This was my turning point. I knew something had to change, and that change started with investing in myself.

I began exploring personal development, reading, attending seminars, and learning from those who had already walked the path I was now embarking on. But it wasn't until I learned public speaking with Jessen James that I began to see the power of personal transformation. Through Jessen, I had the privilege of working with incredible mentors, such as Rob Moore and John McGregor.

I understood the importance of storytelling, not just as a business tool but also as a means for personal growth. I learned that telling my story could be a source of healing, not just for me but for others as well.

I found strength in being real, in telling the truth about what I was going through, and in allowing myself to not have it all together. And, as I did that, I realised something powerful:
People don't want polished perfection. They want truth. They want real stories from real people. They want to know that someone has been through the fire and come out stronger.

Storytelling became my key to connecting with others, inspiring change, and truly finding my voice. It was through sharing my struggles, my vulnerabilities, and my triumphs that I began to heal, and I realised that everyone has a story worth telling.

That's why I wrote my first book, "Left in Peace Not Pieces".

I know you've got a story to tell, too. You've probably faced setbacks. Maybe things didn't go according to plan. There may have been moments when you felt overlooked, unheard, or uncertain about what step to take next. But deep down, you still feel that drive, that pull to create something powerful, something that speaks to your audience and positions you as an authority in your field.

And if you have already tasted success, built your brand, hit milestones, and earned recognition, then you know how important it is to keep evolving. Every great entrepreneur has a moment when they realise that the story that got them here isn't the same one that will take them to the next level. The most impactful brands aren't built solely on strategy; they're powered by story, purpose, and connection.

Your book is about leveraging your experience and knowledge to build authority, attract your ideal clients, and create a lasting impact—whether you're in the room or not. It's about giving yourself permission to step into the spotlight and share your knowledge with the world. It becomes a tool for transformation—not just for your readers but for you, too.

I've seen it firsthand. I've lived it. Writing my book changed my life. Although it had nothing to do with business at the time, it ultimately became a cornerstone of my business, boosted my credibility, and unlocked opportunities I never imagined. I know what it feels like to take your expertise and turn it into something that resonates beyond a conversation or a post.

Now, it's your turn.

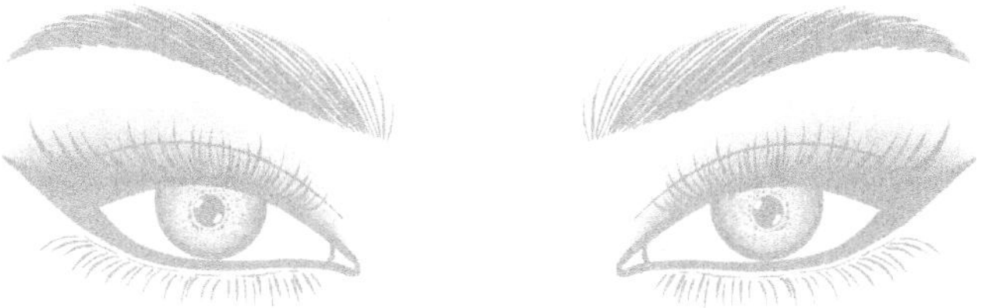

Chapter 2

The Invisible Expert Trap

The Invisible Expert Trap

"Mastery is just the beginning—it's being seen that turns your gift into greatness."

You've done the work. You've put in the hours, served your clients with heart, and mastered your craft. You know your work changes lives, delivers results, and makes a real difference. But here's the frustrating truth:

Being excellent at what you do isn't enough.

Because in today's world, it's not just about what you know —it's about who knows you.
And if no one knows you, no one can hire you, refer you, or quote you. That's the trap. The Invisible Expert Trap. You're highly capable... yet frustratingly overlooked.

Sound familiar?

Perhaps you've watched others in your field—those less experienced and less effective—land the big opportunities. Get the spotlight. Get the clients. Get the recognition. Meanwhile, you're still stuck in the background, hoping your results will speak loudly enough to be heard. They won't. Not unless you give them a voice.

In this chapter, we're going to unpack the painful (but fixable) reality of being the "best-kept secret"—and how to break free. You'll see why visibility isn't just a nice-to-have; it's essential if you want to lead, grow, and serve at scale. And most importantly, you'll discover the most powerful visibility tool at your disposal: your book.

This isn't about self-promotion. It's about stepping into the authority you've already earned—and building the platform that allows others to see what you've been delivering all along.

Let's discuss how to break free from the shadows and step into the spotlight—without compromising or shouting louder. Because you don't need gimmicks.

You just need to be seen.

THE PAIN OF BEING THE "BEST-KEPT SECRET"

If you're reading this, maybe this sounds familiar:

- You're amazing at what you do, but people hire flashier, louder competitors who don't deliver half the value you do.
- You get referrals (thank goodness for that!), but growth is slow—and unpredictable.
- You watch others get invited to speak, featured in media, land book deals...and think, "I could do that. I don't know how to get seen."

It stings, right?

You're not sitting around wishing for fame. You want your work to reach the people it can help. But every time you see someone with half the skill and twice the visibility rise to the top, you start to wonder.

You start wondering: Is it me? Am I missing something?

Let me be clear with you. No, you are not the problem. You're not missing talent. You're missing a platform. And that's a huge difference.

Think about it. If you're doing outstanding work, but no one knows who you are, how will people find you? How will they hire you, recommend you, or buy from you?

It's like you've built a five-star restaurant, but you've forgotten to put up a sign outside. People walk right by. Not because they don't want what you offer but because they don't know it's there. That's what it means to fall into The Invisible Expert Trap.

Here's something no one really talks about. Being invisible doesn't just hurt your business—it messes with your confidence. At first, you tell yourself to be patient. To focus on the work.

You say, "My results will speak for themselves."

But after months—or even years—of being overlooked, something starts to shift. You begin to doubt yourself. You wonder why the opportunities aren't flowing. Why is your inbox quiet? Why you're not getting the same traction as others in your space? It's not because you aren't good enough. It's because you haven't been seen enough.

And being unseen, day after day can chip away at your motivation. You start to shrink a little. You play it safer. You hesitate to share your opinions or your wins because... what's the point, right?

Well, this is the shift I want for you:

- From freelancer to thought leader
- From helping quietly to inspiring loudly
- From waiting for permission to owning your voice

And the best part? You don't need to be famous. You need to be focused.

A clear, compelling book doesn't just build visibility; it also fosters trust. It attracts aligned clients, speaking gigs, media requests, podcast invites, and joint ventures, not by chance but by design.

Your book becomes your calling card, your philosophy, your sales tool, your brand story, your lead magnet, and your legacy. All in one.

YOUR BOOK IS YOUR PLATFORM

Escaping the invisible expert trap isn't about being louder—it's about being undeniable. Many experts become stuck believing, "If only I were more talented, more experienced, or had a bigger network." But that's not the truth.

You're not invisible because you lack talent. You're invisible because you lack a platform.

Talent is everywhere. What's rare—and what truly creates opportunity—is visibility.

And nothing builds authority faster than a published book. Because in the eyes of the world, authors are seen as leaders. Your book instantly transforms you from a "hidden gem" to a recognized expert. It sends a clear message:

- "I know what I'm talking about."
- "I've organized my thinking into a framework that helps others."
- "I have a clear point of view, and I'm willing to share it."

The moment you become an author, people stop questioning your value—and start quoting your insights. Your book Is More Than Words on Paper—It's a Platform of Power that it's your voice amplified. It opens doors—speaking opportunities, media features, client trust, and collaborations follow naturally when you're seen as an authority.

This isn't just marketing—it's transformation.

It's your moment to step out of the shadows and into the spotlight. Your book breaks the "invisible expert" trap wide open. It says, "I have something to say. I've earned my place here."

REAL PROOF

The Story of Loriea Campbell

I had the honour of working with Loriea Campbell, a former contestant on The Great British Bake Off, and a woman with a powerful story to tell. Her name has been featured across major platforms: Channel 4, Smooth Radio, The Mirror, Society of Radiographers, TV Guide, Female First, and GoldDerby. We helped her publish her powerful memoir, Invisible Punches, where she shares her journey with raw honesty—highlighting how her faith, resilience, and passion for empowering others have carried her through life's hardest battles.

To make her message even more impactful, we launched her book on International Women's Day and Human Rights Day —a celebration of courage and visibility.

And the results? Nothing short of extraordinary:

■Invisible Punches became an International #1 Best Seller on Amazon

■ It soared to the top of powerful categories including:

- Human Rights Law
- Marriage and Divorce
- Biographies of British Prime Ministers
- Historical African Biographies

The book held its own alongside titles by Nelson Mandela, surpassing the works of Margaret Thatcher, David Cameron, and Harry Cole.

This is the power of a book done right.

When you write a book, you don't just tell your story.
You give people permission to rise.
You create a legacy that outlives the algorithm.

Remember, visibility is about making your magic available to the people who need it. You're not being self-promotional. You're being generous.

"When you hide your brilliance,
you're doing the world a disservice."

People are out there searching for a guide, a mentor, a voice that makes sense of their struggle.

Why not let it be yours?

VISIBILITY IS NOT VANITY— IT'S STRATEGY.

Let's clear something up: Wanting visibility doesn't make you self-centred. It makes you smart. Visibility is not about ego —it's about access.

It's how people find you, how they trust you, how they choose you over someone else.

And in today's noisy world, being amazing isn't enough. You need to be findable. And more importantly, you need to be unforgettable. That doesn't mean becoming someone you're not. It means letting your true brilliance shine in a way that people can see, feel, and connect with it.

You're creating a doorway that invites people in. Here's a quote from marketing legend Jay Abraham:

> "A book can establish you as an expert in your field faster than any other marketing tool."

That's because a book carries weight. It shows you mean business. And more importantly, it gives people a reason to know, like, and trust you.

Right now, your story may be sitting in your head, in your journal, or scattered across blog posts and Instagram captions. But it's not reaching the people who need it most.

And let's be honest—your story is too valuable to stay small.

So, what do you do?

You stop waiting for permission.
You stop hoping to be discovered.
You build your own platform—and one of the most potent ways to do that is by writing a book.

Because books open doors.

They introduce you as the expert, not just another option. They don't just speak for you—they shout authority. And when you're finally visible, things start to shift: People come to you. Opportunities flow your way. And most importantly—you begin to trust yourself again. Because you're not just good at what you do.

You're finally being seen for it.

ESCAPE THE TRAP

You don't have to stay stuck in the shadows. The moment you decide to write your book, you are choosing to become seen, heard, and trusted.

You're choosing to lead. Let this chapter be your turning point. You are no longer just in business. You are building a brand centred on a book.

So, let's begin the escape. You've got too much value to stay hidden any longer.

Feeling inspired to finally start your book?

If this message spoke to something deep inside you, take the next gentle step.

Go on the link below to explore free resources that walk you through the process—one step at a time.

www.ousha.co.uk

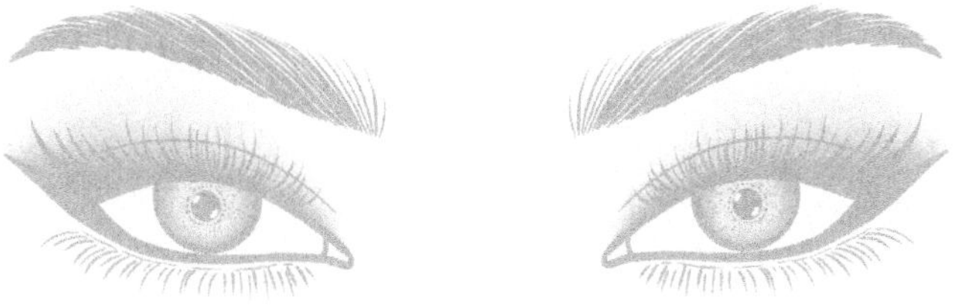

Chapter 3

The Front End of Your Business Starts with a Book

The Front End of Your Business Starts with a Book

"Books aren't just stories. They're portals. They invite people in and build trust."

Too many people treat writing a book like a task to check off their list—something to do once they've "made it", like a trophy on the shelf. However, that mindset overlooks the process's full potential. Writing a book isn't just about putting words on a page or adding another credential to your name. Unlike others, for you, it's not the end goal—it's the beginning. Your book is the launchpad, not the landing.

It gives you visibility, yes. But more than that—it gives you leverage.

"Write the book once. Sell the idea forever."

Your book is the front door to your business; consider it as the first impression of your brand and often the starting point of your client's journey with you. It's not just a product; it's an invitation. A thoughtfully written book pulls readers into your world and starts a relationship that can grow far beyond the last page.

But beyond business, a book is about purpose. It's about telling a story that matters and creating something that lasts. So instead of asking, "How quickly can I get this done?" ask yourself: "What do I want my book to stand for? What message do I want to leave behind?" Because when you write with intention—when you think about the legacy you're building—your book becomes more than a powerful tool.

It becomes something meaningful. Something that leaves a lasting imprint on the people who read it.

Imagine your book like the lobby of a boutique hotel. It sets the tone. It gives people a sense of what they're about to experience. Is your message bold? Soulful? Practical? When someone opens your book, they should feel that from the start. Because this isn't just a business card—it's the most curated version of your brand.

So, think of this chapter as the welcome mat to your brand - the first impression that people will have about you, your message, and what you stand for. And yes, I'm talking about your book.

Now, let's take a step back and examine how this works.

THE "FRONT END" OF YOUR BUSINESS

In marketing, there's a term called "front end." It's all the things that happen before someone becomes a paying customer. Traditionally, this could be free downloads, lead magnets, or a webinar. These strategies were once effective, but the fact is that today's audience has evolved. They're smarter, more selective, and, let's be honest, overwhelmed with content. You know it's true!

But a book? A thoughtfully written book? That's something different. That's an experience.

It's not just a freebie someone grabs to see what you have to offer. It's a commitment from the reader, an investment in themselves and your knowledge. A book signals depth, trust, and value. When someone buys your book, they're not just purchasing a collection of pages; they're stepping into your world. And in a world where people are bombarded with choices, a book stands out.

"The moment someone buys your book, they're no longer just a reader. They're a future client in the making."

When someone chooses to read your book, they're committing. They're investing time and energy to understand your perspective. They're saying: "I want to learn from you."

That's powerful.

And it's why a book doesn't just build awareness—it builds trust. And trust is the foundation of every strong brand.

WHY BOOKS ATTRACT COMMITTED, HIGH-INTENT PEOPLE

Here's something powerful: books attract serious people. These aren't passive browsers; they're seekers—looking for clarity, inspiration, and real solutions.

Think about it. When someone downloads a free checklist or scrolls past a quick video, they might glance at it and move on. But a book? That's a different level of commitment. Whether it's a physical copy or a digital one, reading a book requires time, focus, and intention.

That's why a book is more than just content—it's a decision. When someone chooses to read your book, they're choosing to spend hours with your voice, your story, and your philosophy. That level of engagement builds something far more valuable than clicks or views: trust.

And trust is everything.

When you write a book, you don't just share your expertise—you showcase it. Page by page, you're proving that you know what you're talking about. You're offering value, not in snippets, but in depth. That kind of credibility can't be matched by a single blog post or social media caption.

A book becomes an extension of you—your beliefs, your method, your message. It allows readers to feel like they know you. And once they finish your book, something profound happens: "If this person gave me this much value in a book, imagine what it would be like actually to work with them."

That's the shift— from reader to raving fan; from casual curiosity to serious interest and from stranger to client.

And this is where the real power lies—not in the number of books you sell, but in the number of relationships you start. Once trust is established, the door opens to deeper connections, higher-value offers, and long-term business growth.

This transformation begins with how your book positions you in the reader's mind, not just as a writer but as a guide. As someone worth following. As someone worth investing in.

And it all starts with one book.

"Every great business begins with trust.
Your book is where that trust is born."

FROM READER TO RAVING FAN (AND LIFELONG CLIENT)

Once someone picks up your book, what happens next? Most authors stop here. But you? You're just getting started. You're here to turn readers into clients, clients into advocates and advocates into legacy builders.

This journey has five essential stages.

Stage 1: Awareness (Your Book as the Magnet)

This is where someone first discovers you. They stumble upon your book, hear about it, or see a quote from it on social media.

Your goal? Get the right people to notice your book.

Tactics:

- Be a guest on niche podcasts
- Give away the first chapter for free
- Host a virtual book club or challenge
- Speak at online summits or events

"Your book becomes a lighthouse, drawing in the people you're meant to serve."

Stage 2: Engagement (Your Book as a Mirror)

Once someone starts reading your book, it needs to resonate with them. Your story, your methods, your voice—it all needs to make them feel seen.

Your goal? Deepen the emotional connection.

Tactics:

- Ask reflection questions in the book
- Include QR codes or links to bonus material
- Share real client case studies
- Invite readers to join your email list for tools or templates

"Your words aren't just teaching—they're guiding a transformation."

Stage 3: Nurture (The Bridge Between Book and Business)

Here's where most authors stop. But not you. You'll create momentum by bringing readers into your ecosystem—your newsletters, training, and online community.

Your goal? Keep the connection alive.

Tactics:

- Offer a free video series or workbook that complements the book
- Create an automated email sequence that tells your

deeper story
- Start a private reader group on Facebook or Circle

"Trust grows where the conversation continues."

Stage 4: Offer (Your Book as a Launchpad)

Now they're ready. If they loved the book, and now, they're thinking, "What else does this person offer?" That's your moment to show them.

Your goal? Make the next step clear, exciting and straightforward.

Tactics:
- Include a back-of-book CTA to work with you
- Offer VIP readers early access to coaching spots or programs
- Design a "Book to Brand" sales page that shows how to go deeper

"If your book moved them, they'll want to work with you."

Stage 5: Transformation & Testimony (Your Book Creates Ripple Effects)

Once you've turned a reader into a client. Now it's time to deliver results and celebrate their wins.

Your goal? Turn success stories into brand stories.

Tactics:

- Collect before/after testimonials
- Invite clients to be case studies in future editions
- Feature their wins in your brand story

"Every client becomes a storyteller for your brand."

This isn't just strategy. It's legacy.

"One book can open 100 doors.
One idea can change 1,000 lives."

As those ripple effects build, something else begins to happen: your book starts attracting a different kind of attention—the right kind. People who are ready to invest, ready to grow, and ready to go deeper don't just stumble upon your work—they seek you out.

THE LEGACY MINDSET

Now, let's take a moment to shift your mindset about writing a book.

What do you want your book to stand for?

Most people approach writing with the simple desire to "get a book out there." They think, "I want to write a book." While that's great, I want to challenge you to think bigger.

This is where the magic happens. When you shift from thinking, "I want to write a book", to thinking, "This book will change lives," you change the entire dynamic of what you're about to create.

This isn't just about crafting a few chapters to share your expertise; it's about creating something timeless that will leave a lasting imprint on your readers. When you write with the intention of legacy—when you pour your purpose, passion, and mission into every word—you elevate the value of the entire process, both for you and for your audience.

When you start thinking bigger, everything changes. You'll begin to approach your writing differently. It's no longer just a task to tick off; it becomes an act of service. You're giving something of value to your readers. You're creating a shift in their thinking, their lives, and their businesses. And in doing so, you'll make an impact that reverberates long after your book is published.

Additionally, this mindset shift will fuel you through the writing process and ensure your book stands as more than just a business card; it becomes a tool for transformation.

ALIGNING YOUR BOOK WITH YOUR LIFE'S MISSION AND VALUES

The true power of your book lies in its alignment with your personal mission and values. And the beautiful thing is that's when your message becomes personal, purposeful, and powerful.

When your book reflects who you are—what you believe, what you stand for, and the impact you want to make—it transforms from a simple marketing tool into a living expression of your life's work. It becomes your legacy in written form.

Look at Rich Dad Poor Dad by Robert Kiyosaki. That book wasn't just a bestseller—it was a revolution. Why? Because it aligned so profoundly with his mission to change the way people think about money, wealth, and financial education. It challenged conventional thinking, drew from his own life experiences, and became a global movement—not because it was flashy, but because it was genuine, authentic, and aligned. This is the power of writing a book that's rooted in your truth.

So, what are your core values? What do you believe needs to change in the world? How does your business reflect that belief? And most importantly—how can your book carry that message further?

When your book is anchored in your mission, your readers will feel it. And when they think it, they'll remember you—not just as an author, but as a leader with a message that matters.

This is your opportunity to write something that doesn't just inform... but transforms.

EXAMPLES OF BOOKS THAT CREATED A LEGACY

Let's take a look at a few books that didn't just succeed—they created legacies.

- "Start with Why" by Simon Sinek

Simon didn't just write a book about leadership. He created a movement. The message behind Start with Why tapped into a deep-rooted need for purpose-driven leadership. It turned Sinek into a global thought leader, impacting leaders and organisations around the world.

- "The Lean Startup" by Eric Ries

Eric didn't just give advice on startups; he revolutionized the way entrepreneurs approach business. His book has become a cornerstone of modern business strategy, teaching millions about lean methodology and validating the startup world's need for adaptability and testing.

- "You Are a Badass" by Jen Sincero

This book didn't just motivate women—it empowered them to take charge of their lives and make bold moves. Jen's message of self-belief, empowerment, and unapologetic success became a legacy of its own, inspiring countless readers to rethink their potential.

- "Becoming" by Michelle Obama

Michelle Obama's memoir is more than a personal story—it's a global inspiration. Becoming offered vulnerability, strength, and vision.

It permitted readers to own their stories, find their voice, and stand tall in the face of adversity.

These books did more than make money—they shaped industries, created movements, and left an enduring mark on culture. What you need to understand is that every one of these authors started exactly where you are, with an idea, a message, and a desire to make a difference.

They weren't born bestselling authors. They were individuals who chose to take the initiative.

So don't let their success intimidate you—let it inspire you. If they can build a legacy with their words, so can you.
Your story has power. Your voice has value. And your book? It could be the next one that changes everything.

Now back to you. You've read the benefits. You've seen how a book can transform your brand, elevate your authority, and attract the right people to your business. Now, it's time to take action.

But please don't write a book to check it off your to-do list. Write one that will change your life and the lives of others. A book that not only serves as a tool for building your personal and business brand but one that resonates deeply with your audience. A book that builds trust with every page and positions you as the go-to authority in your field.
It is time for you to write a book that matters.

Are You Ready for This?

If you're hesitating to write that book because you think you're "not ready," flip that script. You're not writing it because you've arrived. You're writing it to begin. To open the door. To invite the right people in.

"Don't wait to be seen as an authority.
Write the book—and become one."

The moment has come. Imagine stepping into a whole new realm of visibility, influence, and authority. And it all starts with the words you write.

But here's the secret: it's not enough to dip your toes in. To harness the full power of your story, you must commit. You must show up every day, sharpen your focus, and pour intentionality into every chapter of the book you're destined to write.

Take Manuel Evaristo Da Luz Gonçalves, author of Dynamic Mindset. When I met him, he told me that he always dreamed of writing a book. My response to him was, "Stop dreaming and start writing". On his 40th birthday, he didn't wait for perfection—he launched his message with crystal clarity and fierce intention. The result? A No. 1 International Best Seller in just a couple of months. His book didn't just share his story; it positioned him as a trusted authority in the field of personal growth.

It is now opening doors to opportunities, client relationships, and impact he once only dreamed of.

The book Dynamic Mindset has officially reached #1 Best Seller on Amazon, not just in one but in five incredible categories! He was at the top-ranking book in:

- #1 Best Seller in Business, Finance & Law Dictionaries
- #1 Professional Purchasing & Procurement
- #1 Fiction About Values & Virtues for Young Adults
- #1 Nonprofit Organisations & Charities
- #1 School & Education Material for Young Adults

And here's the jaw-dropping part: Dynamic Mindset didn't just climb the charts... it soared above the legendary Dr Wayne W. Dyer, the original pioneer of mindset. Imagine that. Beating out a global icon on launch day? Now that's how you celebrate a birthday. But the momentum didn't stop there.

Manuel's book caught the eye of none other than Alfie Best; yes, the Gypsy Billionaire himself who proudly showcased Dynamic Mindset at a significant event. That's next-level visibility. From dream to bestselling reality, from author to authority, from invisible to unmissable.

This is the power of starting.

When you stop waiting and start writing, doors open, connections spark, and the world begins to take notice. Your book becomes more than a story—it becomes a bridge. A bridge between your value and your visibility. Between your message and the people who need it most.

So, ask yourself: Are you ready?

Are you ready to write a book that not only builds your brand but transforms your audience?
Are you ready to create a legacy that will live on long after you've closed the final chapter?

I believe you are. And I know you can do this.
This is your moment.

Don't wait for the "perfect time" or the "perfect idea."

Start writing today, and watch how everything starts to shift. The visibility, influence, and authority you've been dreaming about are waiting for you on the other side of this book.

So, take a deep breath. Picture the person out there who needs your story, your method, your voice. They're waiting at the front door.

Let the book be the key.

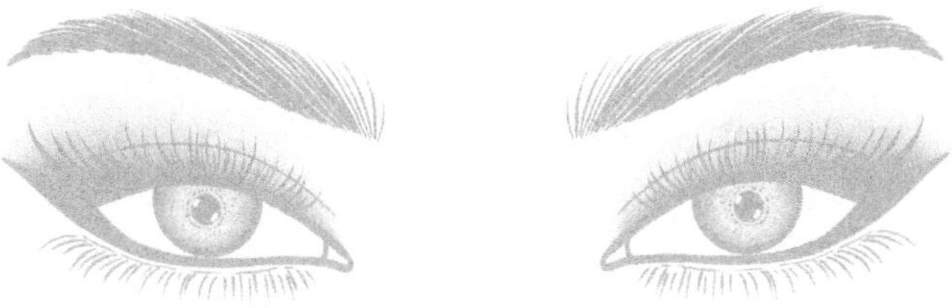

Chapter 4

The Authority Ladder

The Authority Ladder

"People do business with those they know, like, and trust."
– Bob Burg

Let's be honest—being great at what you do isn't enough anymore. You could be the most gifted coach, consultant, therapist, or creative out there. You might have the experience, the heart, the talent. But if your ideal clients don't trust you right away, they won't work with you.
That's the harsh truth.

That's not because they're rude or blind—it's because we're living in a fast-paced, scroll-heavy world. People are skimming, judging, deciding—in seconds. And in those seconds, they're silently asking themselves:

"Can I trust this person?"
"Do they get me?"
"Are they worth my time?"

The problem is that most people are blending in and saying the same things, sharing generic content, and working hard, yet still feeling invisible.

So, how do you go from unknown to undeniable—without spending years grinding it out? The answer is you need a shortcut to trust. You see,

Authority is Earned—But It Doesn't Have to Be Slow!

You do NOT need to spend 10 years grinding just to become known in your field. Sure, authority is something you earn, but you don't need a hundred podcast appearances, a viral TEDx talk, or a massive following to become a respected voice in your industry.

You need the right vehicle—the one that moves you from "best-kept secret" to go-to expert with clarity and speed.

That vehicle is your book.

> "Writing a book is the fastest way to go from unknown expert to undeniable authority."

In this chapter, you'll learn how to build instant credibility with your ideal clients using simple, powerful trust triggers. You'll discover how to stop blending in and start standing out. And you'll see why your book—yes, your book—is the ultimate shortcut to becoming the go-to expert in your space.

So, if you're tired of feeling overlooked, underbooked, or just plain invisible... keep reading.

Because the climb to authority doesn't have to be slow—and you're about to take the express elevator up.

THE ULTIMATE TRUST ACCELERATOR

Imagine trust like a ladder. At the bottom, people don't know you exist. As they climb, they begin to know, like, and eventually trust you. And once they trust you? They invest in you.

But the problem is, most people are stuck at the bottom, shouting up, hoping someone will hear them. Meanwhile, the most innovative entrepreneurs? They build trust triggers into everything they do—especially their book—so ideal clients climb that ladder faster. The goal is to help your ideal clients climb that ladder quickly—from "Who's this?" to "I want to work with them!"—without years of grinding it out in obscurity.

So, how do you earn that kind of instant trust?

Let's break down the three authority accelerators—the core trust triggers that can turn curious readers into committed clients:

1. Testimonials and Social Proof

Nothing builds trust like results.
When it comes to building authority with your book, few tools are more powerful than what other people say about it.

Readers' praise is the trust bridge that connects your words to new audiences. It's one thing for you to say your book is transformative—but it's another thing entirely when a reader, client, or industry peer says, "This book changed how I think," or "This helped me land three new clients." That kind of proof is solid gold.

Every authentic review, every shared result, every social media post where someone's holding up your book and saying, "You need this!" is a rung on your Authority Ladder.

"Nothing sells your services like the results you've already created."

And yes—Ahem, have you noticed? I've included some of that social proof in this book. (Totally on purpose, not just to humblebrag. Okay, maybe a little bit of a humblebrag.) However, it's also a real-time demonstration of how you can achieve the same thing in your book.

Think of testimonials as a bridge between curiosity and confidence. When readers see others' experiences, they begin to believe you can deliver, too.

So, when you write your book, consider including a few of your best testimonials inside the book—at the start, between chapters, or even as a "reader voices" section at the end. That not only builds trust as people read but also shows momentum: this book is already making waves.

REAL CASE STUDY:

From Manuscript to Media

"We are forever grateful for the help and guidance Ousha provided to us. She worked tirelessly to get our book, The Diabetes Solution, published within the required timeframe – and thanks to her expertise, it became an Amazon #1 bestseller in three categories, even ranking above books by Gordon Ramsay and The Hairy Bikers. The success of the book has massively increased our visibility and positioned us as trusted authorities in the wellness industry. Since its release, we've been featured on Sky TV and invited to speak on numerous podcasts. Our YouTube channel experienced massive growth, and we even received an award in recognition of our contributions to health education. Ousha's dedication, professionalism, and supportive approach were instrumental in making all of this possible. We highly recommend her to anyone looking to make a real impact with their book."

You see, don't wait for dozens of reviews to start showcasing social proof. One detailed, heartfelt testimonial beats a hundred vague ones. If someone tells you how your book helped them—even in a casual message—ask if you can use that as a blurb—screenshot kind words. Save LinkedIn shout-outs.

Every little bit helps elevate your credibility.

2. Content Depth That Connects and Converts

Let's be honest—surface-level content is everywhere. You've seen the kind of vague, fluffy, sounds-good-but-says-nothing kind of writing. The type of book you finish and think, "Did I actually learn anything?"

That's why, in the world of authority-building books, depth is a differentiator. It's what separates the forgettable freebies from the books people highlight, quote, and reread. Your audience doesn't need another 200-page pitch. They need clarity, insight, and a sense that you get them.

And yes, you may have noticed again. If this chapter is hitting a nerve, that's because I'm doing exactly what I'm preaching. You're not just reading a book.

You're being guided by someone who's walked the walk.

When you write a book that goes deep—really deep—you do something powerful:

- You show readers that you understand their pain points
- You speak their language and mirror their internal struggles
- You offer practical frameworks, real stories, and actual solutions

When your reader feels like you get them, they're more likely to follow you. That's how trust is built—through relevance, empathy, and insight. Depth proves that you've been where they are. You're not writing from the clouds; you're writing from experience. You're not just guessing—you know.

This is where many would-be thought leaders often fall short. They try to sound smart instead of being useful. Don't try to impress people with big words. Impress them by solving their big problems.

Depth isn't about showing off. It's about showing up for your reader in the moments that matter—with exactly the words they didn't know they needed.

3. Niche Clarity

The fastest way to lose trust is to try and appeal to everyone.
The fastest way to gain it? Speak to someone specific.

So, if you want your book to build authority, start by getting crystal clear on who it's for and what problem it solves. Because,

Vague = forgettable.
Specific = trustable.

Writing for "everyone" is the fastest way to be ignored by everyone. But when your book speaks directly to a particular someone, it becomes irresistible.

So instead of writing a generic "personal development" book that claims to help people "live their best lives" (yawn), say: "This book is for burned-out corporate women who want to shift into heart-led coaching careers—without losing income, confidence, or their sense of identity."

You see, that's clear. That's magnetic. That builds authority. Your book should feel like it was written just for them. When your ideal reader picks it up and thinks, "Wait... this is me," that's when the real magic happens. That's when they trust you, refer you, and buy from you.

Just like this book you're holding isn't for everyone either. It's for experts, entrepreneurs, and changemakers who want to use one book to transform their visibility and authority. (Sound familiar?)

Niche clarity is not about narrowing your impact; it's about clarifying your niche.

It's about sharpening your message so it cuts through the noise. A clearly positioned book doesn't shrink your audience—it helps your actual audience find you faster.

The more clearly your book defines who it helps and how it helps, the more authority you build—before they even finish the first chapter.

WHY A BOOK BEATS EVERY OTHER TRUST TOOL

Well, a book can do for your authority in days that might otherwise take you years.

When someone reads your book, they're spending hours with your voice, your ideas, and your story. That's deep. That's intimate. That's authority. That's a level of trust no Instagram reel can build. And trust is everything. Once trust is established, the door is open for deeper relationships, higher-value offers, and, eventually, long-term business growth.

This is where the real power lies—not in the number of books you sell, but in how you transform readers into loyal followers who are ready to invest in what you offer next. And that transformation begins with how you position yourself in the reader's mind.

"Writing a book is the fastest way to go from unknown expert to undeniable authority." – Me (and thousands of authors who've done it!)

You're not just delivering content; you're delivering experience.

While you sleep, your book is building trust.
While you walk the dog, it's selling your expertise.
While others chase leads, your book is attracting them.

Still not sure what's possible?

Well, you've read my client's testimonial earlier. They didn't just write a book, The Diabetes Solution. —they launched a movement.

- Became Amazon's #1 Bestsellers in three categories
- Ranked above celebrity authors
- Landed features on Sky TV
- Grew their YouTube channel
- Received awards for health education

All from one book.

Why? Because they didn't just publish. They positioned themselves. They built a brand. They delivered trust at scale. You see, their story is proof; the right book, guided by the right strategy, doesn't just make noise; it opens doors, builds legacy, and amplifies your voice far beyond what you thought possible.

But here's something even more personal. When I first published Left in Peace, Not Pieces, I didn't realise the full power of what I was holding.

Back then, I didn't launch it with a business strategy in mind. I wasn't trying to create a brand ecosystem or craft a funnel. I just wanted to share my story and help people heal. And yet, it still drew people to me.

I remember chatting with a woman about my coaching services. As I started to explain what I was doing, she stopped me and said: "Ousha, you don't need to tell me more. I've read your book. I already know you. I'm ready to work with you." That was the moment it clicked. That's the power of a book, my friend.

"A book isn't something you sell—
it's something that sells you."

It sells your experience, your voice, your credibility, and your value. It builds trust and positions you as someone who gets it, who's lived it, who can lead others through it.

Think of it like this:

- While others are still trying to "build their audience," your book is doing the heavy lifting—introducing you, validating you, and proving you know your stuff.
- While others are busy chasing leads, your book is attracting the right ones by speaking directly to their pain points and goals.
- While others are waiting to be picked—by a podcast host, a conference planner, or a media outlet—you've already positioned yourself as an expert who's ready to lead.

"Books don't just share your message.
They prove you've got something worth saying."

You see, when people finish your book, they feel like they know you. They trust you. They're ready to take the next step with you.

No hard sell. No convincing. Just connection.

That's what authority looks like.

AUTHORITY IS A LADDER. YOUR BOOK IS THE ELEVATOR.

You can spend years climbing the ladder one slow rung at a time... Or You can take the elevator.

Your book is that elevator. It gives your audience everything they need to trust you:

- Your story
- Your process
- Your proof
- Your personality
- Your promise

And once trust is built?
Opportunity flows.
Clients say yes quicker.
Referrals come easier
Doors open faster.
You're seen. You're respected. You're in demand.

So, ask yourself:

What would change if your ideal clients saw you as the go-to expert in your space?

Because that's precisely what happens when you write the right book:

- It positions you.
- It elevates you.
- It accelerates your path to impact.

One Last Thing Before We Move On...

You're not just writing a book.
You're building a platform.
You're creating a message that moves people.
You're establishing yourself as someone worth listening to.

In the next chapter, I'll show you how to build that kind of book—step by step.

Not just a book that sounds good...

But one that sells your genius and changes the game.

Let's build it.

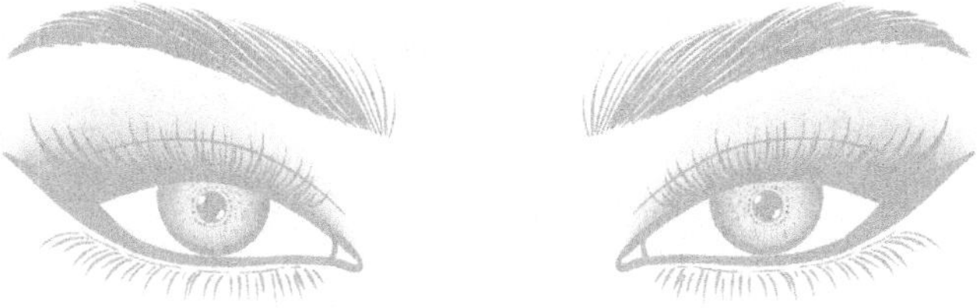

Chapter 5

Choose a Catchy, Outcome-Based Title

Choose a Catchy, Outcome-Based Title

When you're browsing books, what makes you stop scrolling and pick one up?

Is it the cover design, the author's name, or is it the title?

If we're being honest, the title plays a significant role in whether a book catches your attention. You see, your title is more than just the name of your book. It's the first impression you make, the hook that grabs attention, and the promise of what's to come. Think of your title as the cover of a gift. It's the thing that makes people want to open it, unwrap it, and discover what's inside.

Coming up with a title that does all of that can feel tricky. The HOOK formula makes it simple, memorable, and practical to create a title that grabs attention and keeps readers curious. Let's break it down.

- Highlight the Value
- Outcome
- Offer
- Keep It Emotionally Charged

Each part of this formula will guide you in crafting the perfect title for your book. So, let's dive in!

SECTION 1 HIGHLIGHT THE VALUE

Your book title isn't just a name; it's your first impression, and it needs to do some heavy lifting. Before they even open the book, people want to know:

What's in it for me? Will I learn something new? Solve a problem? Shift my mindset?

It should instantly signal that your book offers something relevant, meaningful, and worth their attention. Whether your book provides a powerful insight, a new way of thinking, a skill, or a solution—they should feel that value right from the title.

Remember, your title isn't just a description of the book's contents. It's not a chapter summary.

It's a promise of transformation—the value they'll take away with them.

And when readers sense that value?

They get curious. They lean in. They want to know more.

SECTION 2. OUTCOME

This is where it all comes together. Your title should indicate what transformation your reader can expect. Not a vague idea. A specific, exciting outcome.

Something they can picture, crave, and feel drawn to. Remember, your title isn't about the journey. It's about the destination.

It should say, in effect:
"Read this—and something in your life will improve."

When someone sees your title, they should immediately think: "This book will change something important for me."
That promise is what gets readers excited. It's what turns curiosity into action.
Your title becomes more than just a name. It becomes:

- Your pitch
- Your hook
- Your invitation to a better version of the reader's life

It's like a movie trailer that doesn't give everything away—but gets people excited enough to buy a ticket.

Let's take this a step further with some famous examples of books with powerful, outcome-driven titles.

Notice how they all highlight the benefits clearly:

- Think and Grow Rich by Napoleon Hill

Outcome: Attaining financial and personal success by mastering your mindset. This title doesn't just promise financial wealth—it speaks to the bigger idea of growing in all areas of life. The outcome isn't just about having money—it's about personal growth and mindset transformation. The reader immediately understands that this is about a shift in thinking that leads to success.

- The Power of Now by Eckhart Tolle

Outcome: Finding peace and enlightenment by living in the present moment. Straightforward, isn't it? The title doesn't focus on the methods of mindfulness or meditation; it focuses on the outcome of embracing the present. It speaks directly to anyone seeking peace, offering a tangible promise: live in the now and find peace. No fluff, just the promise of calm and enlightenment.

- The 7 Habits of Highly Effective People by Stephen Covey

Outcome: Achieving effectiveness in personal and professional life. You don't have to guess what this book is about. The outcome is right there in the title: effectiveness. It's a promise that by following these seven habits, you'll notice improvements in both your professional and personal life. The transformation is clear: greater efficiency, productivity, and balance.

- The 4-Hour Work Week by Timothy Ferriss

Outcome: Achieving more with less effort, creating a lifestyle of freedom and productivity. This is like a dream come true for anyone tired of the grind. The outcome is right there: less work, more life. A 4-hour workweek sounds like a fantasy, but the title promises a radical transformation in how you approach productivity and lifestyle. The benefit? More freedom, more time, and still being successful.

- The Miracle Morning by Hal Elrod

Outcome: Transforming your life by implementing a morning routine. A simple promise: transform your life. The focus here isn't just about "getting up early"—it's about the life-changing results that a morning routine can bring. The outcome is an entirely new approach to your day and life, with the morning serving as the starting point for personal transformation.

- Rich Dad Poor Dad by Robert Kiyosaki is another perfect example of an outcome-led title.

Outcome: Gaining financial independence by learning from two different mindsets.

The title 'Rich Dad Poor Dad' grabs attention because it contrasts two opposites: one "rich" and one "poor." The reader is drawn in by the promise of understanding how different perspectives on money can lead to different outcomes. It's simple, memorable, and promises a shift in how we think about money.

<u>Why Outcome-Based Titles Work</u>

Well, I have provided a lot of examples so you can see the pattern for yourself!

Simply put, because it taps directly into what readers want. When readers see a title that promises a specific transformation, they immediately get excited. They can picture themselves achieving that change. Titles that emphasise the outcome show the reader that they're not just buying a book—they're buying a new life, a new way of thinking, or a solution to a problem they're facing.

Think about it: no one buys a book to "learn something." They buy it because they want to change. They want to solve a problem, improve something, or achieve success in a particular area of life. Your title, if done right, acts as the ticket to that change.

The Formula: Simple. Memorable. Powerful.

The best titles do three things:

- Simple: They aren't wordy or complicated. They communicate the promise of transformation in just a few words.
- Memorable: They stick in the reader's mind, making them easy to recall and share.
- Powerful: They create a sense of urgency or desire. The reader can feel the benefit even before they start reading.

When you create a title that speaks directly to the outcome of your book, you make it easier for your readers to visualise the change they'll experience. And when that happens, you make them want to know more, to dive deeper, to leap into their transformation.

SECTION 3: OFFER

Once you've shown the value and highlighted the benefit, the next step is to offer a clear, compelling promise—one that feels personal and powerful. Your title should confidently answer the question every potential reader is silently asking:

"What exactly will this book help me achieve?"

This isn't about summarising what's inside your book—it's about showing them what's on the other side of reading it.

Ask yourself:

- Will they walk away with more confidence?
- Will they finally solve a problem that's held them back?
- Will they start seeing real results where they've been stuck?

Think Promise, Not Process

This is where many authors trip up. They focus on the method or the structure of the book.

But readers don't buy processes. They buy promises.

When someone picks up a book, they're usually looking for help. Relief. A breakthrough. A way out of a challenge they're tired of struggling with.
Your title is your first chance to say: "I see your problem—and here's what your life could look like after reading this."
This is what makes your book irresistible. It's not just a read—it's a transformation.

Think about these bestselling titles:

- "Atomic Habits" promises Tiny changes → massive results.
- "The 4-Hour Work Week" promises More freedom and less work.
- "The Power of Now" promises Inner peace right now.

None of these titles tell you how they'll get you there.
But they all promise a destination readers desperately want.

It's not just a label—it's your first impression, your headline, your hook. It doesn't just land in your reader's mind—it lands in their gut. It sparks emotion. Curiosity. Intrigue. It whispers, "This might be the change you've been looking for." That's the power of tapping into emotion right from the start—because when your title makes them feel something, they're far more likely to trust you, remember you, and take the next step.

It took me years to find the right title for my book—Left in Peace, Not Pieces. And when I say years, I mean it. I wrestled with it. I jotted down ideas, tossed them aside, and then jotted down more, hoping something would click. This book is a profoundly personal journey, one shaped by struggle, healing, and, ultimately, a search for inner peace. But how do you sum all that up in a few words?

It wasn't until one of my good friends—and my brother from another mother, as I always call him—Dr. Ikhenemoh said something to me every single time we ended our conversations, and it finally clicked. He kept saying, "I will leave you in peace, not Pieces". I knew that was the title my story needed. And then one day, it hit me. So, I can't take credit for the title. That honour goes to Dr. Ikhenemoh.

People were drawn to it immediately. It became a conversation starter. And honestly, it did more than just open doors for me.

It brought attention, sparked deeper connections, and, yes, even though my book had nothing to do with my business at the time, it drew a lot of business and notable clients my way. You see, the right title doesn't just sum up your journey; it grabs attention.

Now, back to your book title, here are some tips to Nail Your Title:

1. Keep It Simple, Keep It Memorable. A powerful promise doesn't need to be complex—it needs to stick.
The best titles are:

- Short and sharp
- Easy to remember
- Emotionally charged
- Focused on the result

2. Test It Out: Don't be afraid to test your title on a few people before you commit. Ask your friends, colleagues, or target audience for their thoughts. Does it grab them? Does it make them want to learn more? If not, keep tweaking until it hits just right.

3. Avoid Overused Buzzwords: Words like "mindset" or "hustle" are everywhere. While they may work for some books, try to be different. You want to stand out, not blend in.

REAL CLIENT SUCCESS

Let me show you what's possible when your title hits the mark. I had the honour of working with Rocane Clark, an ambitious entrepreneur with a powerful story. We worked together for just three months—and during that time, he trusted me to guide him through writing and publishing his book: Rock to Riches.

The title was bold, relatable, and promise-driven. It spoke to both his journey and the transformation he offers others.

The result? Rock to Riches became an International #1 Best Seller, surpassing books by Anthony Robbins, Rob Moore, and Robert Kiyosaki—some of the biggest names in personal development and finance.

Top #1 Best Seller Rankings in 6 Major Categories:

- Personal Financial Planning
- Professional Public Finance
- Financial Engineering, National Debt & Deficits
- Debts & Deficits Economics
- Business School Guides
- Multilevel Marketing

And the wins didn't stop there—Rock to Riches continued ranking in:

- Business Economics
- Strategy & Competition
- Financial Aid

This wasn't just a title. It was a movement, a message, and a magnet for growth—both for Rocane's brand and his business.

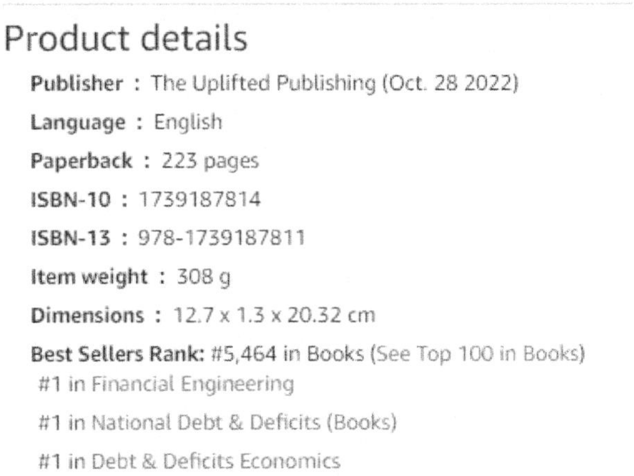

Product details

Publisher : The Uplifted Publishing (Oct. 28 2022)

Language : English

Paperback : 223 pages

ISBN-10 : 1739187814

ISBN-13 : 978-1739187811

Item weight : 308 g

Dimensions : 12.7 x 1.3 x 20.32 cm

Best Sellers Rank: #5,464 in Books (See Top 100 in Books)

#1 in Financial Engineering

#1 in National Debt & Deficits (Books)

#1 in Debt & Deficits Economics

So, how do you create a title that instantly resonates with your audience?

You combine emotion with strategy. The best titles strike a balance between clarity, curiosity, and connection. They evoke a sense of emotion in the reader—while promising a result or transformation.

Here are a few proven formulas to help you brainstorm a title that grabs attention and opens hearts:

1. The "Promise + Audience" Formula
Speak directly to your readers and what they want.
Examples:

- Confidence for Coaches
- Healing for High Achievers
- Leaders Who Love: The Empath's Guide to Leading with Heart

2. The "Result + Timeframe" Formula
Promise a transformation within a certain time.
Examples:

- Find Your Voice in 30 Days
- Six Weeks to Soul-Aligned Success
- Master Your Message in One Month

3. The "How-To" Formula
Classic, clear, and compelling.

Examples:

- How to Build a Business Without Burning Out
- How to Attract Clients Without Feeling Salesy

4. The “X-Step System” Formula

Structure builds trust. Numbers signal simplicity.

Examples:

- The 5-Step Confidence Code
- 7 Shifts to Rewrite Your Money Story
- The 3-Part Framework to Attract Clients Who Say Yes

5. The “Provocative Statement or Question” Formula

Use curiosity and tension to engage the reader emotionally.

Examples:

- You’re Not Lost, You’re Just Hiding
- What If You’re Not the Problem?
- They Told You to Be Quiet—You Wrote a Book Instead

6. The “Metaphor or Wordplay” Formula

Creative titles can become iconic when done well. It's Memorable and brandable.

Examples:

- The Unmuted Life
- Burn the Rulebook
- Brand Like a Rebel

So, as you wrap up this chapter, remember that a powerful title opens doors, turns heads, and gets people curious before they've read a single word.

So, take your time, test a few, and choose one that stirs emotion and captures the heart of your message. Because when your title speaks to the right person in the right way—it doesn't just invite them in. It makes them feel like your book was written just for them.

So, focus on the outcome your reader will get from your book. Think about what transformation your readers are after—whether it's financial freedom, emotional healing, or personal development—and promise that transformation through your title. Keep it clear, keep it compelling, and keep it result-driven.

Your title is your first pitch. Make it count.

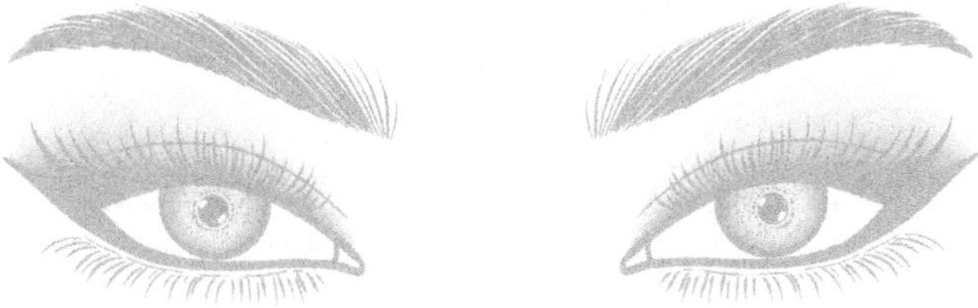

Chapter 6

The Signature System

The Signature System

"Don't just be the expert.
Be the expert with a method." – Unknown

Perhaps you have the skills, experience, training, and a client wins and a heart for real transformation. You've helped people shift their lives, businesses, health, or mindset in powerful ways. You're not just talented; you get results.

But let me ask you this: If someone stopped you today and asked, "What's your method? How exactly do you help people get those results?"
What would you say?

Would you light up and walk them through a clear, confident step-by-step process that shows the power of what you do? Or would you pause and say something like,

"Hmm, well... it depends," or "It's kind of hard to explain"?

If that's you—don't worry. You're not alone.

Most brilliant, heart-driven experts like you operate from instinct. What you do comes naturally. It's personalised. You adapt in the moment.

You tweak things based on what your client needs. And that's beautiful. However, the problem is that what lives in your head can't build your business.

If people can't see your process, they can't understand your value. And if they can't understand your value? They won't fully trust it. They won't refer to it. And they likely won't pay what it's truly worth.

This reminds me of that famous quote from Einstein:

"If you can't explain it simply,
you don't understand it well enough."

Ouch, right? You see when you don't have a straightforward way to show what you do, you blend in. You become "just another coach," "just another consultant," "just another creative." You make it harder for people to choose you—no matter how good you are. Think about it: how many times have you said something like:

- "I just help people."
- "It's hard to explain unless you experience it."
- "Every client is different, so I tailor it every time."

Sound familiar?
Look, flexibility is great. Being client-centered is essential. But if your work is so vague that even you can't explain it clearly... it's a red flag.

Because vagueness kills sales.

It makes people second-guess you. And it keeps you undercharging, overlooked, and undervalued. That's why you need a Signature System.,

- It turns your intuition into a blueprint.
- It turns your gift into something scalable.
- It turns "I kind of get what she does" into "Oh wow, I need that."

And yes—your Signature System becomes the spine of your book. It's the core message that anchors your authority. The thing that makes you unforgettable.

So, in this chapter, we're going to dive into:

- What makes a Signature System truly work
- Why it instantly boosts your credibility
- And how to start creating yours—even if everything you do feels "custom."

You're the expert. You just need a system that shows the world what you already know in a structured way.

Let's build it.

WHAT IS A SIGNATURE SYSTEM?

Your Signature System is the transparent, repeatable process you use to deliver real, consistent results to your clients. It's the step-by-step method that turns your expertise into something tangible—something others can see, follow, and trust.

It's your methodology. Your framework. Your secret sauce. You've got to take it out of your head. It needs to be shaped, polished, and packaged in a way that people can immediately understand. Here is something everyone in business learns the hard way:

"People don't buy vague. They buy clarity."

When you take your knowledge and turn it into a clear, structured process—a system—it instantly changes everything. Suddenly, you're not just "great at what you do."

You're the creator of a method.
A leader with a framework.
A brand with a blueprint.

This clarity does something powerful—it upgrades how people see you. It moves you from "just another expert" to the expert who has a proven way to deliver results. It becomes the backbone of your brand, your book, and your business.

And here's why it matters so much:

"A confused mind never buys.
A clear framework sells for you."

When your potential clients understand your process, their doubts start to disappear. They know exactly what to expect, how the journey will unfold, and why they can trust you to guide them.

Your Signature System becomes the backbone of your entire business—your marketing, your messaging, and most importantly, your book. Your book isn't just words on pages —it's a map of your system, a clear path you've laid out for your readers. It's proof that you've developed a repeatable method for solving problems.

And here's a secret many don't realise: when you communicate your system, you don't just attract clients—you attract the right clients. The ones who resonate with your approach, value your expertise and are ready to say "yes" to working with you.

In other words, your Signature System doesn't just help you close sales—it builds trust, creates authority, and positions you as the go-to expert in your field.

So, if you've been thinking, "How do I stand out in a sea of experts?" or "How do I get people to really understand and value what I do?"

the answer is right here: Build your Signature System.

Make your method visible. Make it memorable. And watch how everything changes.

WHY A SIGNATURE SYSTEM CHANGES EVERYTHING

When you turn your process into a Signature System, you become:

■ Easier to Trust
People feel safer when they can see the path. When you say, "I've got a proven process for this," they lean in. Your work goes from "mystery" to "method."

■ Easier to Refer
If someone says, "I help people transform," it's hard to refer them. But if someone says, "I take burned-out entrepreneurs through my 3-part Reignite Method to get their spark—and profits—back," boom. That's memorable. Shareable. Referrable.

■ Easier to Pay
Look, people don't pay premium prices for random advice or "vibes." They pay for clarity and confidence. A Signature System says: "I know what I'm doing, I've done it before, and here's exactly how I'll do it with you."

That's value. And people pay for value.

In fact, many premium brands and high-ticket programs are simply well-positioned frameworks.

Framework = Focus
Focus = value
Value = Higher Prices

Let's look at some familiar examples:

- Dave Ramsey has the 7 Baby Steps.
- Mel Robbins has the 5 Second Rule.
- Stephen Covey had the 7 Habits of Highly Effective People.

You see, they didn't invent human behaviour or, finance or productivity. They just packaged what they knew into a framework people could follow and pay for.

YOU can have your Signature System too.

HOW TO BUILD YOUR SIGNATURE SYSTEM

Your Signature System can Be Simple. Don't overthink it. Your system doesn't have to be complicated or overly academic. In fact, 3–5 steps is often perfect.

Easy to remember. Easy to teach. Easy to sell.

Here's a refined, step-by-step formula to help you build yours:

<u>Step 1: Reflect on Common Client Struggles</u>

Before you build your solution, you need to deeply understand the problem.
Ask yourself:

- What do clients usually complain about before working with me?
- What's keeping them stuck, frustrated, or overwhelmed?
- What's the situation they're trying to fix, improve, or escape?

Look for emotional language, repeated phrases, and real-world examples. Clarity on the problem sharpens the power of your solution.

<u>Step 2: Think About Your Process</u>

You likely already follow a rhythm, even if it's unspoken.
Ask yourself:

- What are the typical steps I take a client through?
- What do I always start with?
- What do I do in the middle?
- What do I wrap up with?

Your method is probably already there—it just needs structure.

Step 3: Break it Into Phases

Most strong systems have 3–6 clear, teachable phases. Think of it like a client journey:

1. Where they start (problem)
2. What they do with you (steps)
3. Where they end up (result)

For example:

- Align → Activate → Amplify
- Assess → Build → Launch → Scale
- Discover → Declutter → Design

Phases should feel like a path to transformation. Give each phase a name that fits your voice and brand. Don't be afraid to make it memorable, even playful.

Step 4: Name the Whole Framework

This is key. Your framework needs a name—something catchy, clear, and on-brand.

Example: Let's say you're a brand coach for coaches. Your Signature System might be:
Examples:

- The VIBE Method
- The Clear Path Process
- The Soulful Systems Framework

A name turns your steps into a branded intellectual property.

Step 5: Connect Each Phase to a Promise or Result

Don't just name the steps—anchor them in what they deliver.

Example (from The VIBE Method):

- Vision (clarify your brand message)
- Identity (design your visual brand)
- Buzz (build your platform)
- Expression (launch with confidence)

This makes your system outcome-focused, not just activity-based.

Step 6: Test It, Teach It, Tweak It

Creating your Signature System is just the beginning—refining it through real-world use is where the magic happens.

Here's how to bring it to life:

- Test it with clients: Start using your system in 1:1s, workshops, or small groups. See where it flows naturally—and where people get stuck or confused.
- Teach it out loud: Try explaining it to a friend or peer. If you can't articulate it clearly in 90 seconds, it likely needs refining.
- Tweak it with feedback: Pay attention to what resonates most. Do clients light up at a certain step? Does any phase feel unnecessary or repetitive?

Think of this step as the "field testing" phase. The best Signature Systems evolve with experience.

A system that's flexible, responsive, and proven in the field becomes your most powerful asset.

<u>Step 7: Start Using It Everywhere</u>

Now that you've created your Signature System, use it consistently in:

- Sales conversations
- Your website or speaker bio
- Webinars or workshops
- Inside your book
- Client onboarding
- Marketing content

Your system becomes a signature for a reason—use it often and boldly.

WHY YOUR BOOK IS THE BEST PLACE TO SHARE YOUR SYSTEM

No, the exciting part. Your Signature System is the foundation of your book.

Your book becomes more than just your thoughts—it becomes a guide, a roadmap, a tool your readers (and clients) can follow.

- Each chapter can walk through a step in your system.
- You can include real client stories that illustrate each phase.
- You can showcase your process with confidence and clarity.

When a reader finishes your book, they shouldn't just feel inspired—they should feel like they know your method and want to work with you.

THIS IS HOW YOU GO FROM "EXPERT" TO "BRAND"

There are countless smart, talented people out there doing incredible work. But here's the thing—the ones who truly rise to the top? They're not just smart. They're structured and memorable.

They've taken their knowledge and turned it into clear, repeatable systems. Those systems become the foundation for premium offers, group coaching programs, online courses... and, yes, books.

Because your book isn't just another item on your to-do list, it's a powerful tool that takes your expertise and packages it into something tangible, credible, and unforgettable.

When you write your book around your Signature System, you're not just telling people what you do. You're showing them how it works—and why it's worth investing in.

You're turning abstract skills and experience into a straightforward, proven method that delivers results. That's what separates the true experts from the crowd—and transforms them into powerful brands.

Your book becomes the ultimate proof of your authority. It's a physical representation of your system, process, and promise to your clients.

And it doesn't stop there.

That book opens doors to new opportunities. It's your ticket to the big leagues because people don't just want advice—they want guidance from someone who's been there, figured it out, and laid it out clearly.

When you build your brand around a system that's documented in a book, you're creating more than just a business—you're creating a movement. A movement of people who believe in your method, trust your approach and want to follow you because you've made the path clear.

So, remember: being "good" at what you do is just the beginning.

Going from expert to brand means packaging your brilliance into a system, sharing it through your book, and demonstrating to the world why your approach is the best. Your book is more than words—it's the blueprint for your brand's future.

YOUR SIGNATURE SYSTEM IS INSIDE YOU—NOW LET'S MAKE IT VISIBLE

You already have everything you need. Your unique approach, your experience, your way of getting results—it's all inside you, waiting to be named, shaped, and shared with the world.

This moment right here? Consider it your turning point.

From now on, you're not just "someone who helps people" or "an expert who knows their stuff."

- You are the creator of a proven process—a system that others can see, trust, and follow.
- You are a thought leader with a clear framework, someone who brings clarity to confusion.
- You are a brand people remember, respect, and refer to because you've moved beyond vague promises and delivered a clear path to transformation.

And here's the best part: when you build your book around your Signature System, you're doing more than sharing your ideas—you're selling your brilliance.

Your book becomes a beacon, shedding light on your method, message, and impact.

To help you bring your Signature System into clear view, I've included a worksheet on the free resources site: www.ousha.co.uk

Use it to map out your unique steps, define what makes your method special, and craft a memorable name that captures your brand.

This exercise will help you turn the knowledge in your head into a powerful system that your readers—and future clients—can understand, trust, and get excited about. Because your method deserves to be seen. It deserves to be understood. It deserves to be valued. And so do you.

So, take this moment to own your system. Name it. Craft it. Get ready to put it into the hands of readers who are waiting for exactly what you have to offer.

As you can see from the example below, a well-crafted Signature System brings clarity—not just for your clients but for you as well. It's the foundation that turns your expertise into a memorable brand and a powerful message.

This is the same framework I've used with clients who've gone on to write books, launch signature offers, and speak on international stages. One of my clients used this very same approach to publish his book and was soon invited to speak at global events—his method of opening doors he never imagined.

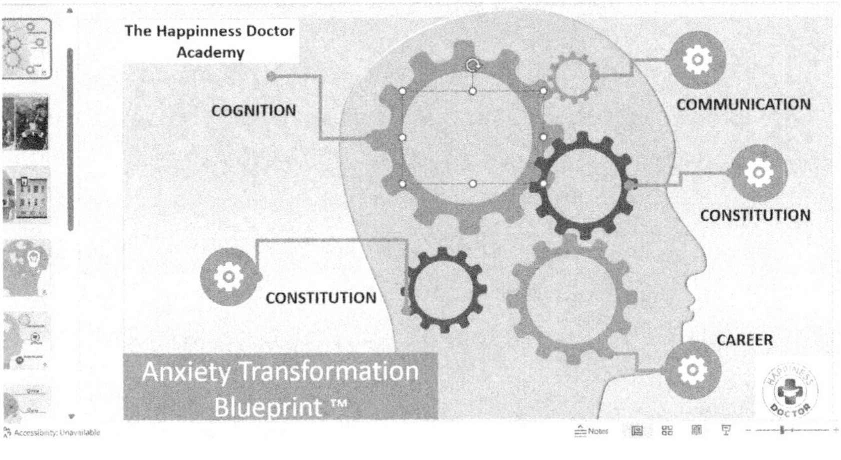

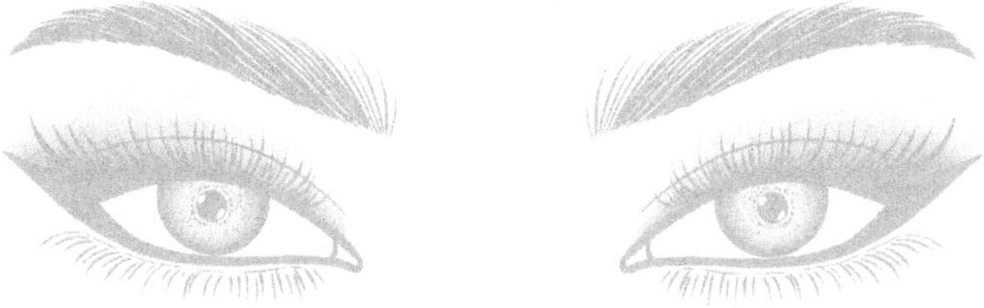

Chapter 7

Monetising Your Book Beyond Sales

Monetising Your Book Beyond Sales

"Don't just write a book—build a business, a brand, and a legacy around it." – Unknown.

Let's stretch the vision. You didn't just write a book to add "author" to your bio., right? By now, you know you wrote it because you recognise the power of your work. Because you have something of great value to say—and something to sell.

The truth is your Book Can Power Your Entire Business.

It's a business model that can open doors to real money, real clients, and real opportunities.
A stage.
A signature.
A sales engine.
A movement waiting to happen.

When done right, your book becomes the seed from which your entire brand ecosystem grows.

So, it's time to stop thinking of your book as a one-and-done project.

Start seeing it for what it is:

- The entry point to your world
- The product that sells your method
- The message that makes your brand unforgettable
- The platform that gives you stage after stage

When you've written the right book, positioned around your Signature System and built with a brand in mind, something shifts:

- You stop chasing clients—and start attracting aligned ones.
- You stop proving yourself—and start being perceived as the authority.
- You stop blending in—and begin building a legacy.

This is the power of a well-placed book inside a well-designed brand ecosystem. In the rest of this chapter, we'll map out exactly how to turn your book into a powerful brand ecosystem—with real-world examples, monetisation models, and simple strategies you can start using right now. Because your book deserves more than online or physical shelf space.

It deserves to build your business, boost your visibility, and change the way people see and pay you.

Let's begin.

YOUR BOOK IS A 24/7 SALES CONVERSATION ASSET

Your book can be your best sales tool you can have.

Why?

Like I explained in Chapter 4, people buy from those they trust. And there's no faster way to build trust than by sharing your insights, your story, and your system in a book.

Imagine this: it's 2:00 AM. You're fast asleep. But on the other side of the world, someone just opened your book for the first time. Within minutes, they're leaning in, nodding along, seeing themselves in your words. By chapter three, they've circled phrases, highlighted strategies, and whispered, "This is exactly what I needed."

That's not just a reader. That's a future client—mid-conversion—while you're in bed, dreaming.

This is the power of a strategically positioned book.

It's not just paper and print—it's presence. It's a trust-building machine. A quiet but unstoppable force that educates, empowers, and enrols—without you having to lift a finger.

Most entrepreneurs chase leads. But authors? They attract aligned opportunities.

Your book speaks on stages you haven't stepped onto yet. It starts conversations before your first handshake. It earns trust in places your marketing can't reach. It doesn't just sell a product—it sells your perspective, your process, and your personality.

People don't just buy books—they buy into worlds.

When someone spends hours reading your story, absorbing your framework, and following your thinking, they form a relationship with you. They trust your expertise. They see your value. And by the time they turn the final page, they don't need convincing—they're already in.

That's not passive consumption. That's conversion in motion. Your book becomes the most competent salesperson on your team:

- It doesn't sleep.
- It doesn't stall.
- It never goes off-brand.
- And it works across time zones, industries, and business models.

In a noisy digital world, attention is currency—and trust is the gold standard. A book earns both. It cuts through the noise. It bypasses scepticism. And it creates a connection that no funnel or ad campaign can replicate.

But more than that, it's a legacy piece, a thought leadership platform, and a credibility amplifier rolled into one. Let it do what no other sales tool can. Your book speaks for you, sell for you, and serve long before you ever say a word. It's your silent, strategic sales conversation that never sleeps.

So, let it work for you, 24/7.

The beautiful thing is that once your book starts working for you, it naturally leads your audience to the next step. It doesn't just build trust—it builds momentum. Every page creates curiosity, and with the right call to action, that curiosity turns into clicks, opt-ins, and booked calls. Your book becomes more than a message—it becomes a magnet for aligned leads who are already pre-sold on you.

So, let your book be your Lead Generation Machine and become your best opt-in offer, whether it's digital or physical.

- Add a free workbook or bonus on the last page to collect email addresses.
- Use it as a lead magnet for Facebook ads or podcast interviews.
- Hand it out at events or conferences.

Readers become leads. Leads become clients.

Don't just say, "Go to my website." Give them something valuable like: "Download the free Bonus Toolkit at [yourURL]."

This turns your readers into relationships.

CASE STUDY: FROM HIDDEN EXPERT TO INTERNATIONAL BESTSELLER & ROI MACHINE

One of my incredible clients, Alex was a cryptocurrency coach sitting on a goldmine of expertise—but practically invisible in his market.

He had the knowledge. He had the results. But he didn't have the positioning that made people pay attention.

That changed when we partnered to craft his signature book, The Crypto Advantage—built entirely around his unique

The results?

■ The book launched as a #1 international bestseller.
■ He transformed the book into a group coaching program that delivered real value.
■ He launched high-ticket services directly aligned with his book's content.
■ He began appearing on top podcast interviews, driving targeted traffic into his funnel.
■ Most importantly—he achieved over 100% ROI within the first 30 days.

This wasn't just a book—it was the lead magnet and authority asset that fuelled his coaching business. When people finally saw his value, they came to him. That's the power of writing the right book.

THE BOOK-TO-BRAND FLYWHEEL

This is the real visibility hack:

- Not just writing a book... but activating it.
- Not just creating content... but building a business.
- Not just being seen... but getting paid for your expertise.

This is about more than authorship—it's about ownership.

And here's a truth most people miss: You don't make money from your book. You make money because of your book. And that starts when you design offers that flow directly from your content.

Your book shows the what.
Your offer delivers the how.

So, if your book discusses mindset breakthroughs, perhaps your offer is a 6-week mindset accelerator.

If your book is about brand clarity, consider offering a one-on-one brand audit and strategy package.

The key is alignment. When the book and the offer align, trust is high, and sales become easier. Then you start turning your ideas into income, your insights into influence, and your book into a brand ecosystem that scales with or without you.

Because when you stop seeing your book as just a product—and start seeing it as the centerpiece of your brand—everything changes.

Imagine a flywheel—one of those big spinning discs used in old-school machinery. Once it starts turning, momentum builds. Each rotation fuels the next. That's exactly how your book can work for you when positioned strategically in your brand.

WHEN POSITIONED INTENTIONALLY, YOUR BOOK BECOMES:

🎤 <u>A signature talk</u>

"The person on stage is the person who gets the clients." – Speaking industry wisdom.

Want to speak on stages, panels, or podcasts? A book is your foot in the door.

Event organisers want two things:

- Someone who knows their stuff.
- Someone who can communicate it.

Your book proves both. You can structure your talk around your Signature System. It's not just a speech—it's a funnel. And every chapter you write is a story waiting to be told from a stage. People don't just buy your book—they buy into your world. By the time they finish reading, they've gotten to know you, trust you, and respect your expertise. You're not selling—they're seeking. And the best part? They're pre-qualified. They already believe in your process. That makes everything easier—from sales to service delivery.

🎓 <u>An online course</u>

People don't just want to read your ideas—they want to live them. By expanding your book's framework into a step-by-step online course, you turn passive readers into engaged students.

This is where transformation happens: readers become action-takers, and your book becomes a pathway, not just a product.

● A high-ticket coaching or consulting offer

Your book outlines your philosophy. Now, imagine a reader reaching the final page and thinking: "I need more. I need them."
That's the bridge to premium offerings—whether it's coaching, consulting, or a group mastermind. Your book has already built the trust. Now, you're simply guiding them to the next level of transformation with you.

🧘 Live retreats or workshops

Some ideas are too powerful to be confined to pages or screens. Your book can be the heartbeat of a live event—a retreat, workshop, or mastermind experience where your philosophy is lived, not just learned. The connections, energy, and breakthroughs that occur in person are irreplaceable. And your book is the magnet that brings people together.

🎧 A podcast or content hub

Podcasting is one of the most powerful tools for long-term visibility. And guess what? You already have the content. Each chapter of your book is a podcast episode in disguise. Each story can become a conversation starter.

Use your book as the backbone of a podcast series, blog, or YouTube channel. Let it guide the themes, guests, and insights you share. That's how you stay top-of-mind.

💼 Licensable IP and certification programs

Have a clear system or framework in your book? That's intellectual property—and it's valuable. You can turn it into a certification program, license it to other coaches, or create curriculum for companies. Suddenly, your message isn't just yours to share—it's a movement that others can join and participate in.

📺 Media exposure & press

Your book is your credibility. Let it open those media doors. And in the eyes of media producers, authors are experts. That means radio, TV, podcasts, articles, and features.
If you've ever dreamed of saying "as seen in..." or being featured in top publications, your book is your key in. Just make sure your message is clear, your pitch is tight, and your positioning is rock solid.

🤝 Sparks Partnerships, collaborations, and brand deals

A well-positioned book attracts more than readers; it attracts allies. Strategic partners. Brands that align with your mission. Collaborators who see synergy in your message.

This is where your book stops working for you and starts working with others. That's exponential growth. You're not just another coach or consultant—you're a published thought leader. People want to collaborate with people who have something of value to offer. And your book? It's a gift that gives back.

💬 And, of course Your Book Attracts Dream Clients

With a clear system, strategy, and structure, your book becomes a bridge to the next level of your business. People don't just buy your book—they buy into your world. By the time they finish reading, they've gotten to know you, trust you, and respect your expertise. You're not selling—they're seeking.

And the best part? They're pre-qualified. They already believe in your process. That makes everything easier, from sales to service delivery.

YOUR TURN: BUILD YOUR ECOSYSTEM

Want help turning your book into an ecosystem of offers and opportunities?

Download the Brand Ecosystem Map worksheet linked at the end of this chapter.

Use it to brainstorm your potential offers, content streams, and speaking angles—all rooted in your book's core message.

And if you're ready to take the next step, I'd love to help you map out your Signature System personally.

Book a free 30-minute strategy session with me (my gift to you for reading this far!).

In this call, we'll sketch the foundation of your method and explore how your book can become a powerful monetisation engine.

https://calendly.com/ousha/15min or visit www.ousha.co.uk

Because your book isn't just a story.

It's your stage, your system, your storefront, and your strategy—all in one.

Let's build the brand that's always been inside you.

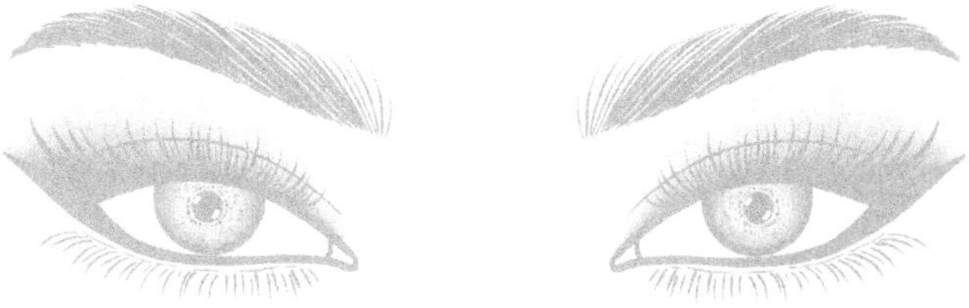

Chapter 8

The Fast and Smart Way to Write Your Book

The Fast and Smart Way to Write Your Book

"A book lives in you already.
All you need is the roadmap to bring it to life."

Writing a book might sound like a long, arduous journey—but it doesn't have to be.

If you follow an innovative, structured process, you can finish your book in a matter of days or weeks, not years. I've seen people spend forever trying to perfect their manuscript only to give up halfway through. Others do manage to finish, but their books barely sell because the process drained all the energy and excitement out of them.

The truth is that writing a book doesn't have to be complicated or time-consuming. You need a method that works. That's what this chapter is all about—a fast, effective, and creative way to bring your book to life.

Let's break it down step-by-step.

Step 1: Start With a Simple Outline

Before you write a single word, you need a plan. Your book outline is like a map—it tells you where you're going and how to get there.

Here's how to do it:

- Grab a notebook, phone, or your favourite writing app.
- Think about the message or story you want to share.
- Jot down every idea, lesson, or point you wish to include.
- Group these ideas into chapters or sections.
- Rearrange them in a logical order—what needs to come first? What builds on what?

Think of your outline like the table of contents of your favourite book. That's all it is—a list of what you're going to talk about in a precise and proper order.

Spend 20 to 30 minutes on this. You don't need perfection—just a solid structure.

Step 2: Speak It Out Loud

Now that you have your outline, here's the fun part: talk your book out loud. That's right—don't type, speak. Use your phone's voice memo app or a free tool like Audacity. Select one chapter or idea from your outline and begin discussing it.

Pretend you're explaining it to a friend over coffee. Be natural; be yourself. Don't worry about sounding perfect. You can clean it up later. Why does this work?

Because speaking is faster than typing, and when you speak, your thoughts flow more freely. You sound more human, more passionate, more real.

Here is a small tip: Break each chapter into a few bullet points to guide your thoughts. This keeps you from going off track.

<u>Step 3: Transcribe Your Audio into Text</u>

Once you've recorded all your chapters, it's time to turn your voice into words.
Some tools do this quickly and affordably. Here are a few options:

- Rev.ai – Fast and accurate, with both AI and human transcription options.
- Otter.ai is a great app that many authors use.
- Descript – A powerful tool that also lets you edit audio and text at the same time.

If the budget is tight, start with the AI option. But if you want high accuracy (and fewer headaches), the human transcription is worth the extra cost.

At the end of this step, you'll have your book in raw written form. It might be messy, but the core ideas are all there.

Step 4: Clean and Restructure with AI Help

Now, it's time to turn your raw transcription into readable content. This is where tools like ChatGPT come in handy. Don't worry—you're not letting AI write your book. You're just using it as a smart editor.

Paste your transcript into ChatGPT and use a simple prompt like: "Can you help rewrite this in clear, book-style language? Keep the meaning and voice, but make it more organised and readable."

Do this chapter by chapter, and you'll quickly have a polished first draft. It's like having a super editor in your pocket—fast, reliable, and always ready.

Step 5: Add Your Voice (Rewrite Like You Talk)

Even after using AI, your book needs your personal touch. Read through the cleaned-up version and rewrite parts in your natural tone. Add stories, examples, and phrases that sound like you.

If your writing sounds like you're having an honest conversation with the reader, you've done it right.

This step might take a day or two, but it's easier than starting from scratch. You already have the material—you're just shaping it into your unique voice.

Step 6: Proofread Like a Pro

Your book is almost ready, but don't skip this crucial step—proofreading. Even a great book can feel unprofessional if it's full of spelling or grammar mistakes. Read through it carefully, or better yet, ask someone else to proofread it for you. Here are your options:

- Do it yourself (if you're confident with grammar).
- Use tools like Grammarly to catch common mistakes.
- Hire a professional proofreader (Fiverr, Upwork, or editorial services).

Spending a little money here can make a big difference in how people perceive your book.

Step 7: Format and Publish

Now that your manuscript is complete, it's time to turn it into a real book. You'll need two things:

1. Formatting – Make it look like a professional book (use fonts, headings, and spacing that are consistent and professional).
2. Cover Design – Create a visually appealing and eye-catching cover.

You can do both of these on your own, but hiring a freelancer can save time and stress. Platforms like Fiverr or 99designs are full of talented designers and formatters.

Once it's all set, you can publish it on Amazon Kindle Direct Publishing (KDP), sell it through your website, or print physical copies.

<u>Bonus Tips for Speed and Success</u>

- Set deadlines: Establish a fixed schedule for yourself. For example, "Finish all voice recordings by Thursday" or "Edit two chapters every weekend."
- Don’t chase perfection: A done book is better than a perfect idea stuck in your head.
- Stay excited: Keep reminding yourself why this book matters. Who are you helping? What’s the purpose?

FINAL THOUGHTS

Your Book Is Closer Than You Think!

Writing a book doesn’t have to be a long, painful process. You don't need to lock yourself away for months or be the next Hemingway. You need a clear system—a way to capture your ideas quickly, shape them into a message, and deliver them to the world. This process has helped countless authors create books fast—and it can work for you, too.

f you stay focused, speak from the heart, and trust the process, your book could be finished in a couple of weeks.
So what are you waiting for?

Let’s get writing.

If you've made it this far, chances are you're not just thinking about writing a book — you're ready to build something meaningful with it. I want you to know you don't have to do it alone. Whether you're still shaping your ideas or already envisioning the impact your book will have, I'd be honoured to walk beside you in this next chapter.

This isn't about pressure or a pitch — it's simply an open invitation to take what's already inside you and bring it to life with clarity, confidence, and momentum. If it feels aligned, let's connect.

Together, we'll turn your book into the brand, business, and legacy you know you're meant to build.

A SPECIAL GIFT JUST FOR YOU

As a heartfelt thank you for investing your valuable time with me, I'm giving you FREE access to my exclusive online workshop — usually priced at £197.

Inside this workshop, I'll share my powerful T7 Step Signature System — the exact method that has helped "ALL" my authors become #1 International Bestsellers and leverage their books to build high-impact, high-income brands.
This workshop is packed with insider tips, actionable advice, and the secrets top authors use to skyrocket their book sales. No strings attached.

Ready to take the next step?

Claim your free workshop here: www.ousha.co.uk

SPECIAL INVITATION

If reading this book has sparked something in you — a desire to finally share your story, elevate your brand, and turn your message into meaningful impact — I want to personally invite you to work with me.

Whether you're at the beginning of your journey or ready to publish your legacy work, I help entrepreneurs, leaders, and changemakers turn their ideas into powerful books that build credibility, create authority, and open new doors in business and life.

If you're ready to take the next step and if you'd like me to personally help you get kick-started, point you in the right direction, and answer your questions, you can book a call with me:

https://calendly.com/ousha/15min

I'd love to support you on your journey and explore how your book can change everything.

Alternatively, email me directly at success@ousha.co.uk

Your voice matters. Your story deserves to be heard.

Here's what one of my clients had to say about the experience:

"Ousha is an absolute gem and an absolute star when it comes to helping you not just find your voice, but package it up into a book that can completely change your business and completely change your life. She's so good at what she does that I trusted her with helping me write and publish my own book, my very first book. And please understand that I've been in my industry for the last 10 to 12 years.

I've dominated my industry as a speaker, I've been international, I've done it all, and my brand is very, very precious to me, and I trusted her to do something that I want you to consider doing. Take a story and share it with the world. It can completely flip your business upside down. It can completely open up new doors for you, and it will give you so much more credibility. And I thought I had credibility until I got my book done.

Your book will amplify you or amplify your message, and it will help you reach out to more people who need to hear your voice. If you get a chance to do that, grab it with both hands, I promise you your future self will thank you for it."

– Jessen James, international speaker, TV personality (Channel 5's Rich House, Poor House), and business mentor

ABOUT THE AUTHOR

Having spent the majority of her life in the United Kingdom, the Mauritian-born Ousha Demello was a former Business Lecturer and worked in the educational sector for over fifteen years, only to have minus in her bank account every month. She then decided to go into entrepreneurship.

She is now an inspirational Business Trainer, International Public Speaker, No 1 International Bestselling Author & Publisher, a wife and a proud mum.

She is also a multiple Business Award Winner who draws on her own personal experiences to help others achieve success. She has trained thousands of people in business, has impacted many lives and helps people turn their knowledge into an income. Her clients praise her for her ability to inspire them to reach their full potential and make their dreams a reality.

Through her tumultuous journey of pain and emotional abuse in her former marriage, Ousha found a renewed sense of purpose and inner strength. Turning her traumatic experiences into a catalyst for change, she penned the powerful book, 'Left in Peace not Pieces', to share her story and provide a guiding light for others facing similar hardships.

Recognising the transformative power of storytelling, Ousha extended her passion beyond her own writing, offering support and guidance to help others find their voice and share their stories too. Her unwavering dedication serves as an empowering reminder that through courage and resilience, we can rise above adversity and inspire change in the world.

This is what she believes:

Your story is your power. Own it. Share it. Shape the world with it.

CONNECT WITH OUSHA DEMELLO

Email:success@theupliftacademy.com /success@ousha.co.uk

Website: www.ousha.co.uk

LinkedIn: www.linkedin.com/in/oushademello

Facebook: https://www.facebook.com/OushaK

Instagram: https://www.instagram.com/oushademello

Book: https://mybook.to/LeftinPeaceNotPieces

Book a Free Strategy Call: https://calendly.com/ousha/15min

"Don't wait for the world to discover you. Build something so powerful it can't be ignored."

THE UPLIFTED
PUBLISHING

Printed in Dunstable, United Kingdom

64669599R00077